THIS BOOK BELONGS TO:

_____

_____

Shop our other books at
www.sillyslothpress.com

For questions and customer service, email us at
support@sillyslothpress.com

JOKE 1

WHAT DO YOU CALL A SNORING BULL?
A BULL-DOZER.

JOKE 2

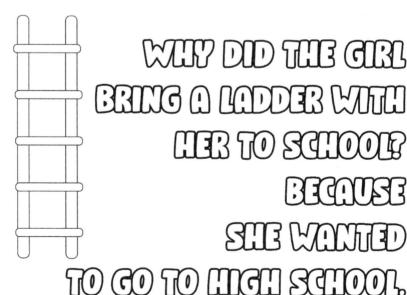

WHY DID THE GIRL BRING A LADDER WITH HER TO SCHOOL?
BECAUSE SHE WANTED TO GO TO HIGH SCHOOL.

JOKE 3

WHAT DID
THE BABY CORN
SAY TO THE MAMA
CORN?
WHERE
IS POP CORN?

JOKE 4

WHAT DID
ONE SNOWMAN
SAY TO THE
OTHER?
DO YOU SMELL
CARROTS?

JOKE 5

WHY DID THE BANK
ROBBER NEED
TO TAKE
A SHOWER?
HE WANTED
TO MAKE
A CLEAN GETAWAY.

JOKE 6

WHAT DO YOU CALL
A BEAR WHO
DOESN'T HAVE
ANY EARS?
A "B"!

JOKE 7

WHAT DO YOU CALL TWO WITCHES WHO SHARE AN APARTMENT? BROOM-MATES.

JOKE 8

NAME A KIND OF TREE THAT FITS IN YOUR HAND? A PALM TREE!

JOKE 9

WHAT DO YOU CALL A WASHED-UP VEGETABLE? A HAS-BEAN.

JOKE 10

WHY SHOULDN'T YOU GIVE ELSA A BALLOON? BECAUSE SHE WILL LET IT GO.

JOKE 11

WHAT DID THE DALMATIAN SAY AFTER DESSERT?
THAT HIT THE SPOT!

JOKE 12

WHAT TIME IS IT WHEN THE CLOCK STRIKES 13?
IT'S TIME TO GET A NEW CLOCK.

JOKE 13

WHAT IS A WITCH'S BEST SUBJECT IN SCHOOL? SPELLING!

JOKE 14

HOW EXPENSIVE IS IT FOR A PIRATE TO GET HIS EARS PIERCED? ONLY A BUCK-AN-EAR.

JOKE 15

WHY DID THE BOWLING PIN HAVE SUCH A ROUGH LIFE? HE WAS ALWAYS GETTING KNOCKED DOWN.

JOKE 16

WHAT SOCIAL MEDIA APP DOES THANOS USE? SNAP CHAT.

JOKE 17

WHAT DO YOU CALL A COW THAT IS ALL OUT OF MILK? A MILK DUD.

JOKE 18

WHY CAN'T YOU HEAR A PTERODACTYL USING THE BATHROOM? BECAUSE THE "P" IS SILENT.

JOKE 19

NAME AN ANIMAL THAT IS ALWAYS AT A BASEBALL GAME?
A BAT.

JOKE 20

WHAT DO YOU CALL A MARRIAGE BETWEEN TWO SPIDERS?
A WEBBING.

JOKE 21

WHAT IS A MUMMY'S FAVORITE KIND OF MUSIC? WRAP.

JOKE 22

WHY DO DUCKS HAVE TAIL FEATHERS? TO COVER THEIR BUTTQUACKS.

JOKE 23

WHERE DOES THANKSGIVING COME AFTER CHRISTMAS? IN THE DICTIONARY.

JOKE 24

WHAT IS A GHOST'S FAVORITE DESSERT? I SCREAM.

JOKE 25

DO YOU WANT
TO HEAR A JOKE
ABOUT PIZZA?
NEVER MIND,
IT'S TOO CHEESY.

JOKE 26

WHAT DID THE FASHION
DESIGNER WEAR
TO THANKSGIVING
DINNER?
A HAR-VEST.

JOKE 27

WHAT'S EVEN WORSE THAN FINDING A WORM INSIDE OF YOUR APPLE? FINDING HALF A WORM.

JOKE 28

WHAT IS TOUGH, RED, AND BAD FOR YOUR TEETH? A BRICK.

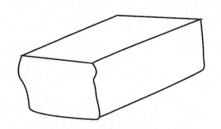

JOKE 29

WHAT WAS THE FIRST ANIMAL IN OUTER SPACE? THE COW THAT JUMPED OVER THE MOON

JOKE 30

WHAT DID ONE VOLCANO SAY TO THE OTHER VOLCANO? I LAVA YOU!

JOKE 31

WHAT DO GHOSTS USE TO WASH THEIR HAIR? SHAM-BOO.

JOKE 32

WHAT DO BIRDS GIVE TO TRICK-OR-TREATERS ON HALLOWEEN? TWEETS.

JOKE 33

DO YOU KNOW WHY
WE PUT CANDLES
ON THE TOP
OF BIRTHDAY
CAKES?
BECAUSE IT'S HARD
TO LIGHT THEM
FROM THE BOTTOM.

JOKE 34

HOW DO
BILLBOARDS
COMMUNICATE?
SIGN LANGUAGE.

JOKE 35

WHERE CAN YOU LEARN HOW TO MAKE ICE CREAM? SUNDAE SCHOOL.

JOKE 36

WHY ARE FISH THE SMARTEST ANIMALS IN THE OCEAN? BECAUSE THEY LIVE IN SCHOOLS.

JOKE 37

ARE BLACK CATS REALLY BAD LUCK? ONLY IF YOU ARE A MOUSE.

JOKE 38

WHY WAS THE WEIGHTLIFTER FRUSTRATED? SHE WORKED WITH A BUNCH OF DUMBBELLS.

JOKE 39

WHAT IS THE SKY'S FAVORITE GAME? TWISTER.

JOKE 40

WHAT DID THE FARMER CALL THE DAIRY COW WHO WAS OUT OF MILK? AN UDDER FAILURE.

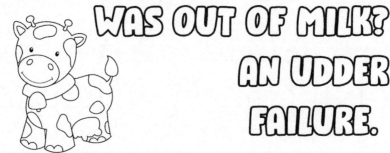

JOKE 41

HOW DO COWS CELEBRATE DECEMBER 31ST?
AT A MOO YEAR'S EVE PARTY.

JOKE 42

WHEN DOES A CUCUMBER TURN INTO A PICKLE?
WHEN IT GOES THROUGH A JARRING EXPERIENCE.

JOKE 43

WHY IS IT A BAD IDEA TO TELL SECRETS IN A CORNFIELD? THERE ARE TOO MANY EARS.

JOKE 44

HOW DOES A LAMB SAY MERRY CHRISTMAS? FLEECE NAVIDAD.

JOKE 45

WHY DID THE SNAKE CROSS THE ROAD? TO GET TO THE OTHER SSSIDE.

JOKE 46

WHAT KIND OF MUSIC DO SODAS LIKE? POP.

JOKE 47

WHAT IS A COMPUTER'S FAVORITE THING TO EAT? COMPUTER CHIPS!

JOKE 48

WHAT DO BASEBALL TEAMS HAVE IN COMMON WITH CAKES? THEY BOTH NEED A GOOD BATTER.

JOKE 49

WHY WOULDN'T THE CLAM SHARE HIS DESSERT? BECAUSE HE WAS A LITTLE SHELLFISH!

JOKE 50

WHAT SHOULD YOU DO IF SOMEONE IS RUDE AND ROLLS THEIR EYES AT YOU? ROLL THEM BACK.

JOKE 51

WHY DID THE BABY
RASPBERRY
START TO CRY?
BECAUSE
HER PARENTS
WERE IN A JAM.

JOKE 52

HOW DO YOU
MAKE
A LEMON DROP?
JUST
LET IT FALL.

JOKE 53

WHAT IS SOMETHING THAT FALLS IN WINTER BUT NEVER GETS HURT? SNOW!

JOKE 54

WHAT IS A VAMPIRE'S FAVORITE PET? A BLOOD HOUND.

HOW CAN YOU STOP
AN ASTRONAUT'S
BABY FROM
CRYING?
YOU JUST ROCKET!

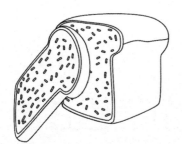

WHAT DOES
BREAD
DO ON ITS DAY OFF?
LOAF AROUND.

JOKE 57

WHAT KIND OF NUT HATES MONEY?
CASH-EW

JOKE 58

WHAT DID THE LEFT EYE SAY TO THE RIGHT EYE? BETWEEN US, SOMETHING SMELLS!

JOKE 59

WHERE DO PENCILS GO WHEN THEY NEED A VACATION? PENCIL-VANIA.

JOKE 60

WHAT IS THE BEST TREAT TO EAT AT THE PLAYGROUND? RECESS PIECES.

JOKE 61

WHAT WEATHER IS WORSE THAN RAINING CATS AND DOGS? HAILING TAXIS!

JOKE 62

KNOCK KNOCK. WHO'S THERE? INTERRUPTING PIRATE. INTERRUPTING PIR— YARRRRRR!

JOKE 63

HOW DOES THE MOON CUT HIS HAIR? ECLIPSE IT.

JOKE 64

WHAT CANNOT HEAR EVEN THOUGH IT HAS EARS? A CORNFIELD.

JOKE 65

WHAT DID JILL TELL JACK AFTER THEY ROLLED DOWN THE HILL?
I THINK I SPILLED THE WATER

JOKE 66

WHY DO SEAGULLS FLY OVER THE SEA?
BECAUSE IF THEY FLEW OVER THE BAY, THEY WOULD BE BAYGULLS.

JOKE 67

WHAT DID THE PLATE SAY TO THE CUP? DINNER IS ON ME!

JOKE 68

WHAT'S GREEN AND HAS THE POWER OF FLIGHT? SUPER PICKLE!

JOKE 69

WHAT WAS THE REACTION
TO BENJAMIN FRANKLIN
DISCOVERING ELECTRICITY?
EVERYONE
WAS SHOCKED!

JOKE 70

NAME SOMETHING
YOU CAN YOU CATCH,
BUT NEVER THROW?
A COLD!

JOKE 71

HOW CAN YOU TELL IF THE OCEAN IS FRIENDLY? IT WAVES!

JOKE 72

WHAT DO YOU DO WHEN YOU RUN OUT OF ROOM FOR YOUR PIGS? BUILD A STY-SCRAPER.

JOKE 73

WHAT DID THE FISHERMAN SAY TO THE MAGICIAN? PICK A COD, ANY COD.

JOKE 74

CAN A CHICKEN FLY HIGHER THAN MOUNT EVEREST? YES, BECAUSE A MOUNTAIN CAN'T FLY AT ALL.

JOKE 75

HAVE YOU HEARD THE ROOF JOKE? NEVER MIND, IT'S OVER YOUR HEAD.

JOKE 76

WHY DID THE MUFFIN GO TO THE DOCTOR? BECAUSE HE FELT CRUMMY.

JOKE 77

WHAT DO YOU CALL
A DROID THAT
TAKES
THE SCENIC ROUTE?
R2 DETOUR.

JOKE 78

WHAT KIND OF LUNCH
DO MOMS
NEVER PREPARE
IN THE MORNING?
THEIR OWN.

JOKE 79

WHAT DID ONE DNA
STRAND ASK
IN THE DRESSING
ROOM?
DO MY GENES
LOOK OK?

JOKE 80

WHY DID THE BAKER
PUT THE CAKE
IN THE FREEZER?
TO ICE IT.

JOKE 81

LEARNING THE BEST WAY TO COLLECT TRASH WASN'T DIFFICULT... I JUST PICKED IT UP AS I WENT ALONG.

JOKE 82

WHICH SIDE OF A BIRD HAS THE MOST FEATHERS? THE OUTSIDE.

JOKE 83

WHAT DID THE BANANA SAY TO THE CAT? NOTHING. BANANAS CAN'T TALK!

JOKE 84

WHAT HAS FOUR WHEELS AND FLIES? A GARBAGE TRUCK!

JOKE 85

HOW DO YOU
FIX A BROKEN
PUMPKIN?
WITH
A PUMPKIN PATCH.

JOKE 86

WHAT IS A TIGER'S
FAVORIT
COLOR?
PURRR-PLE.

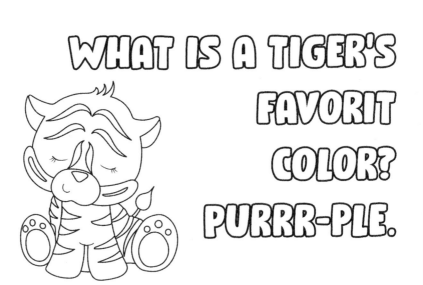

JOKE 87

WHY DID THE PRISONER THROW THE WATCH OUT THE WINDOW? BECAUSE HE WANTED TO SEE TIME FLY!

JOKE 88

WHAT KIND OF ANIMAL DRESSES UP AND HOWLS? A WEARWOLF.

JOKE 89

ARE VAMPIRES GOOD AT MATH? NOT UNLESS YOU COUNT DRACULA.

JOKE 90

WHAT DO YOU CALL A DOG MAGICIAN? A LABRACADABRADOR.

JOKE 91

WHY DOESN'T ANYONE TALK TO OVALS OR CIRCLES? BECAUSE THERE IS NO POINT.

JOKE 92

WHEN DOES A JOKE TURN INTO A "DAD" JOKE? WHEN THE PUNCHLINE IS A PARENT.

JOKE 93

HOW DO YOU TELL
IF A CAR
IS THINKING?
WHEN
YOU SEE ITS
WHEELS TURNING.

JOKE 94

WHAT MAKES
A TISSUE DANCE?
A LITTLE
BOOGIE

JOKE 95

HOW CAN A BABY TELL YOU SHE HAS A WET DIAPER? SHE WILL SEND YOU A PEE-MAIL.

JOKE 96

WHAT DO YOU CALL TWO BIRDS WHO ARE IN LOVE? TWEETHEARTS!

JOKE 97

WHAT DO YOU CALL QUESO THAT'S NOT YOURS? NACHO CHEESE!

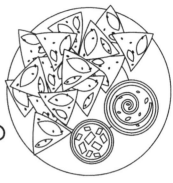

JOKE 98

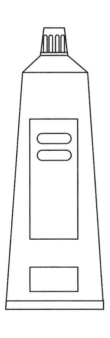

WHAT MUSICAL INSTRUMENT CAN YOU FIND IN THE BATHROOM? A TUBA TOOTHPASTE.

JOKE 99

HOW DO MOUNTAINS STAY WARM IN WINTER? SNOWCAPS

JOKE 100

WHAT DID TARZAN SAY WHEN HE SAW THE ELEPHANTS COMING? "WATCH OUT FOR THE ELEPHANTS!"

JOKE 101

WHY IS IT THAT YOUR HAND CAN'T BE 12 INCHES LONG? BECAUSE THEN IT WOULD BE A FOOT.

JOKE 102

HOW CAN YOU TELL IF SOMEONE IS A GOOD FARMER? HE IS OUTSTANDING IN HIS FIELD!

JOKE 103

HOW DID THE SNOWMAN LOSE A FEW POUNDS? HE WAITED FOR THE WEATHER TO WARM UP.

JOKE 104

WHEN YOU TAKE YOUR WATCH TO THE SHOP TO BE REPAIRED, DON'T PAY UP FRONT... WAIT UNTIL THE TIME IS RIGHT

JOKE 105

WHO IS A GHOST'S TRUE LOVE? HIS GHOUL-FRIEND.

JOKE 106

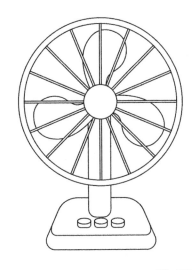

WHY WAS THE STADIUM SO WINDY? THERE WERE HUNDREDS OF FANS INSIDE.

JOKE 107

WHY ARE GHOSTS SUCH BAD LIARS? YOU CAN SEE RIGHT THROUGH THEM.

JOKE 108

WHAT IS CRUNCHY, FAST, AND LOUD? A ROCKET-CHIP!

JOKE 109

WHAT DID THE MAMA
BUFFALO SAY TO
HER SON WHEN
SHE DROPPED
HIM OFF
AT CAMP?
BISON!

JOKE 110

WHAT ANIMAL
CAN YOU ALWAYS
FIND AT A
SOFTBALL GAME?
A BAT!

JOKE 111

WHY DID
THE STUDENT
EAT HER HOMEWORK?
BECAUSE THE TEACHER
SAID IT WAS
A PIECE OF CAKE!

JOKE 112

WHICH CANDLE
BURNS LONGER,
A GREEN OR A PINK?
NEITHER.
THEY BOTH
BURN SHORTER.

JOKE 113

WHAT IS THE BEST WAY TO OPEN A BANANA? WITH A MON-KEY!

JOKE 114

WHAT TYPE OF BUILDING HAS THE MOST STORIES? THE LIBRARY!

JOKE 115

WHAT DO YOU GET WHEN SANTA BECOMES A DETECTIVE? SANTA CLUES.

JOKE 116

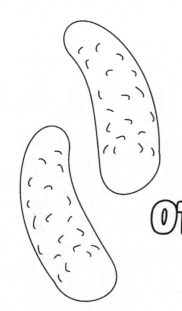

WHAT DID ONE PICKLE SAY TO THE OTHER PICKLE? DILL WITH IT.

JOKE 117

WHAT DID THE NOSE SAY TO THE FINGER? QUIT PICKING ON ME!

JOKE 118

WHY DID THE GOD OF THUNDER NEED TO STRETCH AFTER HIS WORKOUT? HE WAS THOR.

WHY DO WHALES LIVE IN SALT WATER? BECAUSE PEPPER MAKES THEM SNEEZE.

WHAT DO YOU CALL A DEPRESSED STRAWBERRY? A BLUEBERRY.

JOKE 121

WHY DID THE BANANA GO TO THE HOSPITAL? BECAUSE IT WASN'T PEELING WELL.

JOKE 122

WHY ARE ZOOKEEPERS UNTRUSTWORTHY? THEY SPEND TOO MUCH TIME WITH CHEETAHS.

JOKE 123

WHY DIDN'T THE TEDDY BEAR WANT DINNER? HE WAS ALREADY STUFFED!

JOKE 124

WHY WAS THE BROOM FRAZZLED WHEN HE WAS LATE? BECAUSE HE OVER-SWEPT!

JOKE 125

WHY DIDN'T THE LAMP SINK WHEN IT FELL IN THE WATER? IT WAS TOO LIGHT.

JOKE 126

WHY DID THE BICYCLE FALL DOWN? BECAUSE IT WAS JUST TWO-TIRED!

JOKE 127

WHY DO MERMAIDS SWIM IN SALTWATER? BECAUSE PEPPER WATER IS TOO SPICY!

JOKE 128

WHY WAS 6 SCARED OF 7?

BECAUSE 7, 8, 9

JOKE 129

NAME SOMETHING THAT GETS WETTER THE MORE IT DRIES. A TOWEL.

JOKE 130

WHY DID THE SKELETON SKIP THE DANCE? BECAUSE HE HAD NO BODY TO DANCE WITH.

JOKE 131

WHY IS CINDERELLA BAD AT BASKETBALL? BECAUSE SHE'S ALWAYS RUNNING AWAY FROM THE BALL!

JOKE 132

HOW DID THE QUARTER OUTSMART THE NICKEL? IT HAD MORE CENTS.

JOKE 133

WHAT DO SPRINTERS EAT BEFORE THEY RACE? NOTHING. THEY FAST.

JOKE 134

WHAT DO YOU CALL THE HORSES THAT LIVE RIGHT NEXT DOOR? YOUR NEIGHBORS!

JOKE 135

WHAT IS A COBRA'S FAVORITE SUBJECT IN SCHOOL? HISSSSS-TORY

JOKE 136

WHAT DOES A GHOST USE TO DO HER HAIR? SCARESPRAY.

JOKE 137

WHAT DO YOU CALL A DUCK THAT GETS STRAIGHT A'S? A WISE QUACKER.

JOKE 138

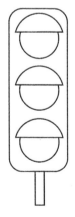

WHY WAS THE TRAFFIC LIGHT MAD? BECAUSE EVERYONE WAS LOOKING AT HER WHEN SHE WAS CHANGING.

JOKE 139

WHAT DO YOU CALL A FAKE NOODLE? AN IMPASTA.

JOKE 140

"HOW IS THAT NEW DINER ON THE MOON?" "FOOD WAS GREAT, BUT THERE REALLY WASN'T ANY ATMOSPHERE."

JOKE 141

WHY DID
THE CHEF THROW
BUTTER?
BECAUSE
HE WANTED
TO SEE A BUTTERFLY!

JOKE 142

WHAT IS THE BEST
WAY TO STOP A BULL
FROM CHARGING?
TAKE AWAY
ITS CREDIT CARD!

JOKE 143

HOW DO BEES BRUSH THEIR HAIR? WITH HONEYCOMBS!

JOKE 144

HOW CAN A SCIENTIST MAKE SURE HER BREATH IS FRESH? WITH EXPERI-MINTS!

JOKE 145

WHAT DID THE PLUNGER SAY TO THE TOILET? YOU LOOK A BIT FLUSHED.

JOKE 146

HOW MUCH DOES A PIRATE PAY FOR CORN? A BUCK-ANEER.

JOKE 147

HOW CAN
YOU TELL THE DIFFERENCE
BETWEEN A PIANO
AND A FISH?
YOU CAN TUNE
A PIANO
BUT YOU CAN'T TUNAFISH

JOKE 148

WHY SHOULDN'T
YOU TELL A JOKE TO
A PIECE OF GLASS?
IT WOULD
CRACK UP.

JOKE 149

WHAT IS THE BEST WAY TO TALK TO A GIANT? USE BIG WORDS!

JOKE 150

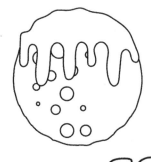

WHERE DO STEAKS GO DANCING? A MEATBALL

JOKE 151

WHAT DO YOU CALL A BOOMERANG THAT DOESN'T COME BACK? A STICK.

JOKE 152

WHEN YOU SEARCH FOR SOMETHING, HOW COME IS IT ALWAYS IN THE LAST PLACE YOU LOOK? BECAUSE WHEN YOU FIND IT, YOU STOP LOOKING!

JOKE 153

WHAT KIND OF HAIRCUTS DO BEES GET? BUZZZZCUTS!

JOKE 154

NAME A KIND OF WATER THAT CAN'T FREEZE. HOT WATER.

JOKE 155

WHERE WOULD YOU FIND A HIPPOPOTAMUS? THE SAME PLACE YOU LEFT HER!

JOKE 156

WHY DIDN'T THE SKELETON GO TO THE PARTY? HIS HEART WASN'T IN IT.

JOKE 157

WHAT DID THE TOAD ORDER AT THE RESTAURANT? A BURGER AND A LARGE CROAK!

JOKE 158

WHERE DID THE CATS GO FOR THEIR FIELD TRIP? TO THE MEW-SEUM.

JOKE 159

NAME SOMETHING THAT GOES UP, BUT NEVER COMES DOWN. YOUR AGE.

JOKE 160

WHY DID THE PONY GET SENT TO HIS ROOM? HE WOULDN'T STOP HORSING AROUND!

JOKE 161

WHAT DO YOU CALL BROTHERS WHO LOVE MATH? ALGEBROS.

JOKE 162

HOW MANY FAMOUS MEN AND WOMEN WERE BORN ON NEW YEAR'S? NONE, ONLY BABIES.

JOKE 163

WHY DID
THE BICYCLE
GET IN TROUBLE?
HE SPOKE
TOO MUCH.

JOKE 164

WHAT TIME
IS IT WHEN A BALL
GOES THROUGH
THE WINDOW?
TIME TO GET
A NEW WINDOW.

JOKE 165

WHAT WAS THE BALDING SEA CAPTAIN VERY WORRIED ABOUT? CAP SIZES.

JOKE 166

HOW ARE FALSE TEETH LIKE THE MOON? THEY COME OUT AT NIGHT!

JOKE 167

NAME A ROOM THAT DOESN'T HAVE ANY DOORS OR WINDOWS. MUSHROOM.

JOKE 168

WHY DON'T ELEPHANTS CHEW BUBBLE GUM? OF COURSE THEY DO! JUST NOT IN PUBLIC.

JOKE 169

WHAT MAKES AN OCTOPUS LAUGH? TEN-TICKLES!

JOKE 170

WHERE DO SANTA'S ELVES VOTE? THE NORTH POLL

JOKE 171

WHAT DO YOU CALL A BEAR WHO LOST ALL OF HIS TEETH?
A GUMMY BEAR.

JOKE 172

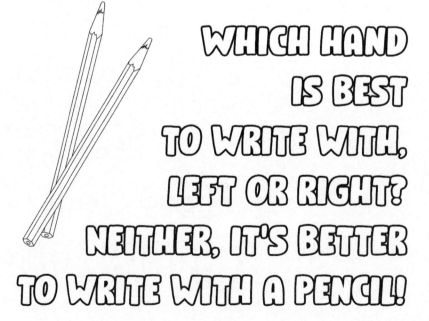

WHICH HAND IS BEST TO WRITE WITH, LEFT OR RIGHT? NEITHER, IT'S BETTER TO WRITE WITH A PENCIL!

JOKE 173

WHAT DO YOU CALL A SLEEPING DINOSAUR? A DINO-SNORE!

JOKE 174

WHY WAS THE NEW PENGUIN SOCIALLY AWKWARD? BECAUSE HE DIDN'T KNOW HOW TO BREAK THE ICE.

JOKE 175

WHY DID
THE DINOSAUR
CROSS THE ROAD?
BECAUSE
THE CHICKEN
WASN'T BORN YET.

JOKE 176

WHAT DID THE ROCK
SAY TO THE GEOLOGIST?
PLEASE
DON'T TAKE
ME FOR GRANITE!

JOKE 177

WHAT DO SANTA'S ELVES LEARN IN SCHOOL? THE ELF-ABET.

JOKE 178

WHY DID THE BOY CROSS THE PLAYGROUND? TO GET TO THE OTHER SLIDE.

JOKE 179

WHAT DO YOU CALL A COW WITH NO LEGS? GROUND BEEF!

JOKE 180

WHAT'S THE DIFFERENCE BETWEEN BOOGERS AND BRUSSEL SPROUTS? KIDS DON'T EAT BRUSSEL SPROUTS!

HOW DO YOU GET ON A SQUIRREL'S GOOD SIDE?? ACT NUTTY!

WHY DID THE PICTURE TRY TO ESCAPE FROM JAIL? BECAUSE IT WAS FRAMED!

WHAT DO YOU CALL A CLOUD'S UNDERWEAR? THUNDERWEAR.

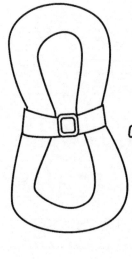

WHAT DID THE ZERO SAY TO THE EIGHT? NICE BELT!

JOKE 185

WHAT DO YOU GET FROM A PAMPERED COW? SPOILED MILK.

JOKE 186

HOW CAN YOU STAY WARM IN ANY ROOM NO MATTER WHAT? GO TO THE CORNER, IT'S ALWAYS 90 DEGREES.

JOKE 187

WHAT DOES IT SOUND LIKE WHEN A COW BREAKS THE SOUND BARRIER? COW-BOOM!

JOKE 188

WHY DID THE RABBIT GO TO THE BARBER? TO CUT HIS HARE.

JOKE 189

WHERE DO COWS GO FOR A DATE NIGHT? THE MOO-VIES

JOKE 190

WHY DID THE COOKIE GO TO THE HOSPITAL? HE WAS FEELING PRETTY CRUMMY.

JOKE 191

WHY DO THE BEST GOLFERS WEAR TWO PAIRS OF PANTS? IN CASE THEY GET A HOLE IN ONE.

JOKE 192

WHAT HAPPENS WHEN YOU CROSS A SNOWMAN WITH A VAMPIRE? FROST-BITE!

HOW DOES
A MUMMY
START A LETTER?
TOMB
IT MAY CONCERN...

WHAT DID
THE RABBIT
TELL HIS WIFE
ON THEIR
ANNIVERSARY?
HOPPY ANNIVERSARY.

JOKE 195

WHAT DID
ONE MATH BOOK
SAY TO
THE HISTORY
BOOK?
I'VE GOT
SO MANY PROBLEMS.

JOKE 196

WHAT ROOM
DOES A VAMPIRE
NOT NEED?
A LIVING
ROOM.

JOKE 197

WHY DID THE BUBBLE GUM CROSS THE ROAD? IT WAS STUCK TO THE CHICKEN'S FOOT!

JOKE 198

WHAT IS MESSY, BLUE, AND SMELLS LIKE RED PAINT? BLUE PAINT.

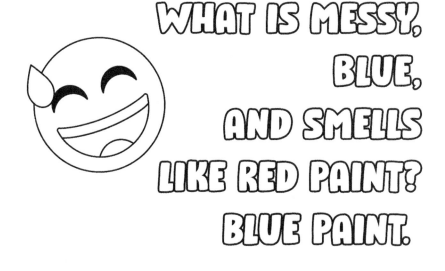

JOKE 199

WHAT IS HAIRY, BROWN, AND WEARS SUNSCREEN? A COCONUT ON VACATION.

JOKE 200

WHAT WILL YOU ALWAYS GET ON YOUR BIRTHDAY? A YEAR OLDER.

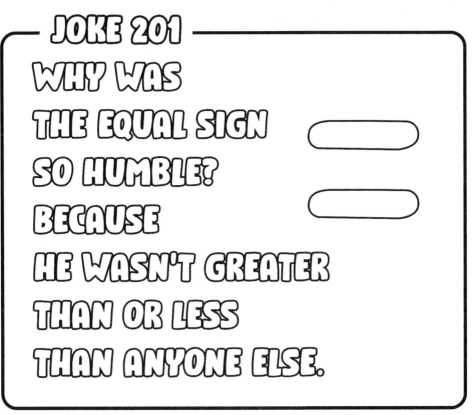

JOKE 201

WHY WAS THE EQUAL SIGN SO HUMBLE? BECAUSE HE WASN'T GREATER THAN OR LESS THAN ANYONE ELSE.

JOKE 202

WHAT WAS THE KITTEN'S FAVORITE MAGAZINE? A CAT-ALOGUE.

JOKE 203

WHAT DID THE POLICEMAN SAY TO HIS BELLY? FREEZE! YOU'RE UNDER A VEST.

JOKE 204

HOW COME THE OBTUSE TRIANGLE IS ALWAYS WRONG? BECAUSE IT IS NEVER RIGHT.

JOKE 205

HOW COME THE FRACTION WAS SO NERVOUS ABOUT MARRYING THE DECIMAL? BECAUSE HE DIDN'T WANT TO HAVE TO CONVERT.

JOKE 206

WHAT TIME IS IT WHEN PEOPLE ARE THROWING TRASH AT YOU? TIME TO DUCK.

JOKE 207

WHY COULDN'T THE PONY SING KARAOKE? SHE WAS A LITTLE HORSE.

JOKE 208

WHAT SOUND DO PORCUPINES MAKE WHEN THEY HUG? OUCH!

JOKE 209

WHAT SHOES DO PRIVATE INVESTIGATORS LIKE TO WEAR? SNEAK-ERS

JOKE 210

WHERE DOES A SNOW LEOPARD KEEP HIS MONEY? IN A SNOW BANK.

JOKE 211

WHERE CAN YOU FIND A DOG WITH NO LEGS? RIGHT WHERE YOU LEFT HIM!

JOKE 212

WHAT DID THE MAMA ELEPHANT SAY TO HER CHILDREN WHEN THEY WERE MISBEHAVING? TUSK, TUSK.

Printed in Great Britain
by Amazon